Put Beginning Readers on the Right Track with
ALL ABOARD READING™

The All Aboard Reading series is especially designed for beginning readers. Written by noted authors and illustrated in full color, these are books that children really want to read—books to excite their imagination, expand their interests, make them laugh, and support their feelings. With fiction and nonfiction stories that are high interest and curriculum-related, All Aboard Reading books offer something for every young reader. And with four different reading levels, the All Aboard Reading series lets you choose which books are most appropriate for your children and their growing abilities.

Picture Readers
Picture Readers have super-simple texts, with many nouns appearing as rebus pictures. At the end of each book are 24 flash cards—on one side is a rebus picture; on the other side is the written-out word.

Station Stop 1
Station Stop 1 books are best for children who have just begun to read. Simple words and big type make these early reading experiences more comfortable. Picture clues help children to figure out the words on the page. Lots of repetition throughout the text helps children to predict the next word or phrase—an essential step in developing word recognition.

Station Stop 2
Station Stop 2 books are written specifically for children who are reading with help. Short sentences make it easier for early readers to understand what they are reading. Simple plots and simple dialogue help children with reading comprehension.

Station Stop 3
Station Stop 3 books are perfect for children who are reading alone. With longer text and harder words, these books appeal to children who have mastered basic reading skills. More complex stories captivate children who are ready for more challenging books.

In addition to All Aboard Reading books, look for All Aboard Math Readers™ (fiction stories that teach math concepts children are learning in school); All Aboard Science Readers™ (nonfiction books that explore the most fascinating science topics in age-appropriate language); and All Aboard Poetry Readers™ (funny, rhyming poems for readers of all levels).

All Aboard for happy reading!

For my favorite little monsters,
Daniel, Micah, and Noah—D.S.

To Patty Lynn, drawn together!—A.S.

1020715

Monstrous thanks to Nily, the Gruens of Newton, and the Steinbergs of Chicago for their help and support—D.S.

Look for the funny rat hiding on every page!

Text copyright © 2004 by David Steinberg. Illustrations copyright © 2004 by Adrian Sinnott. All rights reserved. Published by Grosset & Dunlap, a division of Penguin Young Readers Group, 345 Hudson Street, New York, New York 10014. ALL ABOARD POETRY READER and GROSSET & DUNLAP are trademarks of Penguin Group (USA) Inc. Printed in the U.S.A.

Library of Congress Cataloging-in-Publication Data

Steinberg, David, 1962–
   The Monster Mall and other spooky poems / by David Steinberg ; illustrated by Adrian Sinnott.
      p. cm. — (All aboard poetry reader. Station stop 2)
   ISBN 0-448-43543-8 (hardcover) — ISBN 0-448-43542-X (pbk.)
   1. Halloween—Juvenile poetry. 2. Supernatural—Juvenile poetry. 3. Children's poetry, American. [1. Horror—Poetry. 2. Halloween—Poetry. 3. Humorous poetry. 4. American poetry.] I. Sinnott, Adrian C., ill. II. Title. III. Series.
   PS3619.T47618M66 2004
   811'.54—dc22
                              2003026555

ISBN 0-448-43542-X (pbk)   10 9 8 7 6 5 4 3 2 1
ISBN 0-448-43543-8 (GB)   10 9 8 7 6 5 4 3 2 1

THE MONSTER MALL

AND OTHER SPOOKY POEMS

BY DAVID STEINBERG
ILLUSTRATED BY ADRIAN SINNOTT

Grosset & Dunlap • New York

GROSS FOOD COURT

Krispy Skreamers

Coffin Shop

Ice Cream Bones

Boo-Ritos

Witches Brew

Some monsters go scare-boarding.

Some play boo-sketball.

But me, I get my monster kicks

Down at the Monster Mall.

4

It's fun just monster-watching.

It's my ghoul-friends' favorite sport!

We meet for scumburgers and flies

Inside the Gross Food Court.

We watch ghosts eat boo-ritos.

Skeletons munch ice cream bones.

The witches sip their steamy brews

While yapping on spell phones.

The vampires suck their lattes

In the trendy coffin shop,

While zombies chomp on crawlers

At the Krispy Skreamer stop.

Next up: It's bargain-haunting—

We scare up some monster sales . . .

See, look—we each got bracelets

That go <u>perfect</u> with our tails!

The mummy at the counter

Spritzes us with Eau de Smelle,

While baby headless horsemen

Spin aboard the scare-ousel.

No way! There in the Scare Salon,

Guess who I just saw?

The Wolfman—with a fur-cut

And a stylin' maniclaw!

Is that the Loch Ness Monster

Picking pennies from the pond?

Hold on—I think that's Dracula

In Blood, Bats, and Beyond!

Oh, <u>rats</u>! Mom's here to get me—

We were having such a ball!

Gotta run . . . see you tomorrow—

You can find me at the mall!

12

HENRY THE HUNGRY SKELETON

Meet Henry, the hungry skeleton.

He's hungry <u>all</u> the time . . .

For breakfast he eats twenty pies—

From kiwi to key lime.

For lunch he gulps down jelly beans—

Washed back with soda pop.

For dinner he slurps ice-cream cones—

Each flavor in the shop.

And for dessert, a crate or two

Of chocolate-chip shortbread—

But still, he's <u>always</u> hungry

When it's time to go to bed!

You see, when you're a skeleton,

The food just bounces out.

It slips between your ribs and spine

And tumbles all about.

So all the food that Henry eats

Is there on Henry's floor.

And, sadly, hungry Henry

Will be hungry evermore!

FRANKENFOOD

There was a lonely doctor

Who lived all by himself.

One evening, in his kitchen,

His eyes fell on his shelf.

Then a bolt of lightning lit

His food in all its glory.

"AHA!" he shrieked and brought that food

To his la-bor-a-tory!

He took a HEAD of lettuce,

And was ready to begin.

A HEART of palm, fish FINGERS,

Angel HAIR, some onion SKIN,

The EYES from a potato,

Two tasty EARS of corn,

The NAVEL from an orange,

And—young FRANKENFOOD was born!

This homemade friend smiled and said,

"Wow—I feel incredible!"

The doctor had missed dinner,

And thought, "He looks so edible."

And though his tummy rumbled,

He tried hard to be polite,

Until he couldn't help himself

And asked for one wee bite.

"No thanks, doc!" said the creature.

"I don't care to be a snack."

He whisked off to the kitchen.

In a blink, he bobbled back.

He held a steaming platter

Heaped with chocolate mint soufflé.

"My goodness!" said the doctor.

"I've created a GOURMET!"

"With your talent and my brains, kid,

There are places we can go!"

So they started up a restaurant

And a cable cooking show!

Franken-magazines and cookbooks

Set the bar for taste and style,

While their line
of Franken Kwik-E-Meals

Soon filled the frozen aisle.

Chef Frankenfood was all the rage,

A star in no time flat,

While Doc lived ever after—

Healthy, wealthy, and quite fat.

So when you're sad or lonely,

Here's the moral of the story:

Just take your food and head straight

For your <u>own</u> la-bor-a-tory!

THE WEREBABY

If you are faint of heart,

This poem is not for you.

It's such a spooky, creepy tale,

You'll wonder if it's true.

But just about a year ago—

Midnight on Halloween—

The strangest baby boy was born

That you have <u>ever</u> seen . . .

The moon loomed round and full

On that windy, starless night,

And what the doctor saw then

Made him run away in fright!

By the cold light of the window,

The parents took one look

And stood without a word to say—

They simply stared and shook.

What <u>was</u> it that they saw there?

Was it human? Well, maybe . . .

You see, upon that table

Was a tiny <u>werebaby</u>!

He waved his little furry arms

And kicked his furry feet

And howled a furry howl

That shattered windows down the street.

And though his startled parents
Didn't know quite what to do,
They rocked him in their arms until
He cooed a furry coo.
The werebaby looked up at them
With furry baby eyes—
And they just <u>knew</u> they loved that boy
In any shape or size.

Next morning, when they woke up

(Though I know this will sound weird),

The werebaby was <u>gone</u>!

But he hadn't disappeared . . .

He'd turned into a normal boy,

All cute and pink and bright—

The parents thought they must have had

A scary dream last night!

But only one month later—

As the old clock struck midnight—

They heard a horrid howl

And fumbled for the light.

And there, between the burp cloths

And the blankies in his bed,

Guess who was back to see them,

With his little furry head!

Those parents were <u>so</u> tired

That they started howling, too!

They picked their wee werebaby up

And all three cried,

"Ar-ROOOOOOOOOOOOO!"

Since then, each month at midnight,

You can hear their ghastly croon . . .

Beware—you'd better plug your ears

When you see a full moon!

IT'S TOUGH FOR GHOSTS THESE DAYS

It's tough for ghosts these days.

I tell you, it's not fair!

It used to be so easy

To find someone to scare.

But nowadays I pop up

And sound my spooky cry—

And no one even <u>notices</u>!

I watch folks rush right by!

They're busy with their big-shot phones

And flashy music toys.

These kids today—they frighten <u>me</u>,

They all make so much noise!

And so that brings me to my point.

I'm glad I spotted you—

Yeah, <u>you</u> there, with your quiet book,

I just came to say . . .

BOOOO!